# Print Handwriting Workbook for Young Teens

Practice Workbook with Fun Space Facts that Build Knowledge in a Young Teenager

Print Handwriting Workbook for Young Teens: Practice Workbook with Fun Space Facts that Build Knowledge in a Young Teenager

*Dear friend,*

*I hope you will enjoy this installment of our "Print Handwriting Workbook for Young Teens" series. This edition revolves all around the fascinating and intriguing world that lies in outer space.*

*Warmly,*
*Ellie Roberts*

# Introduction to Print Handwriting

The goal of this workbook is to help you develop or improve your print handwriting skills. It is designed for beginners and intermediates since it mostly focuses on the writing in print style of entire words and sentences.

This book does, however, contain a short practice section for each letter. This overview includes recommendations on how each letter should be written. The rest of the workbook contains fun facts about outer space.

Each exercise is composed of two sections. The first section contains specific words extracted from the sentence and written with a traceable print font. The second section contains a worksheet designed for the sentence to be rewritten in its entirety.

While I highly endorse cursive handwriting because of its scientifically proven benefits. Print handwriting doesn't go without its merits. It can help you develop a neat and legible writing style. It's therefore important, in my opinion, to master both cursive and print handwriting styles. This workbook focuses on the latter.

The facts inside this book can improve your knowledge about the world we live in and can lead to meaningful discussions with friends and family. All that while also improving your handwriting skills.

## Happy Practicing!

# Print uppercase letters

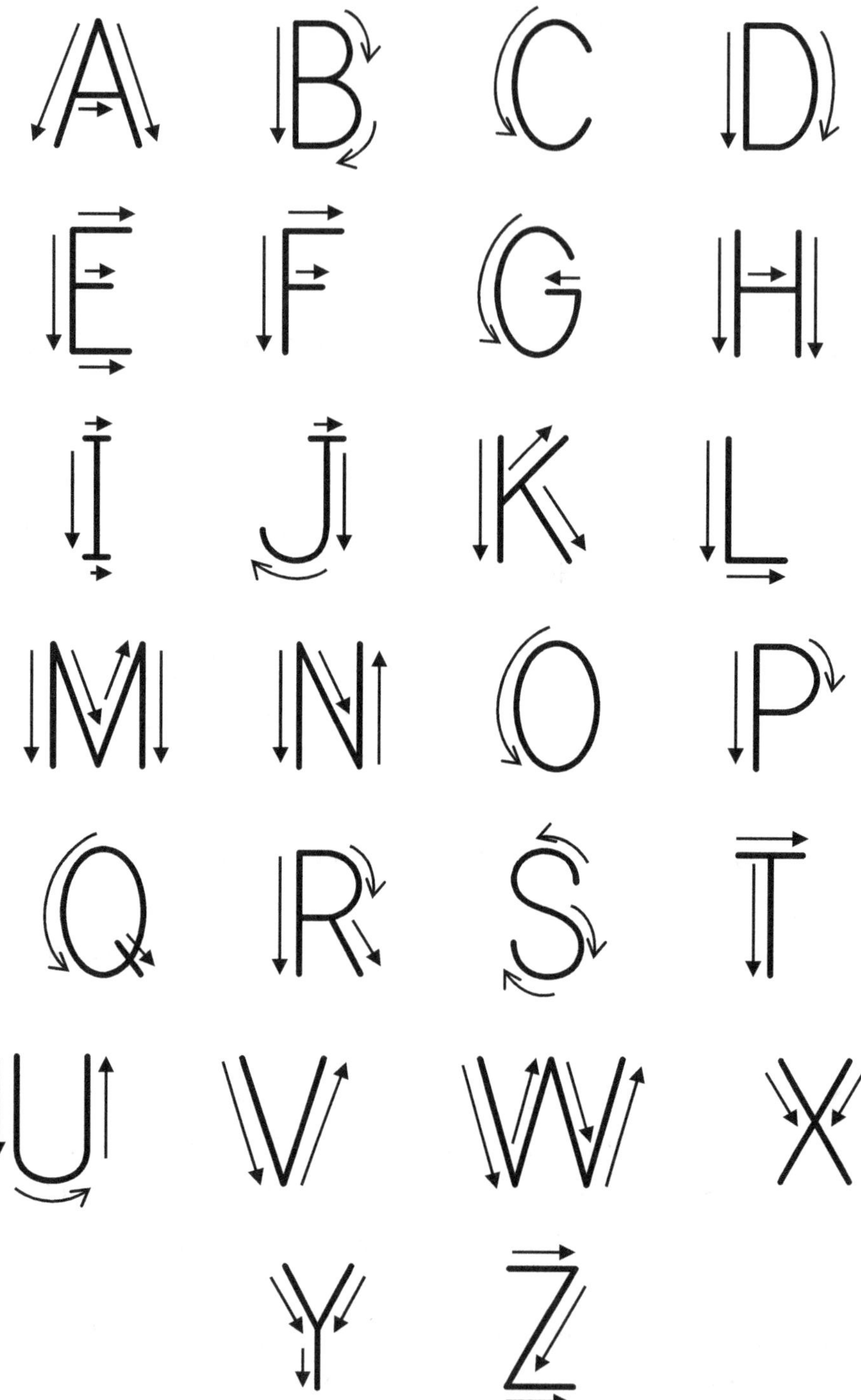

# Print lowercase letters

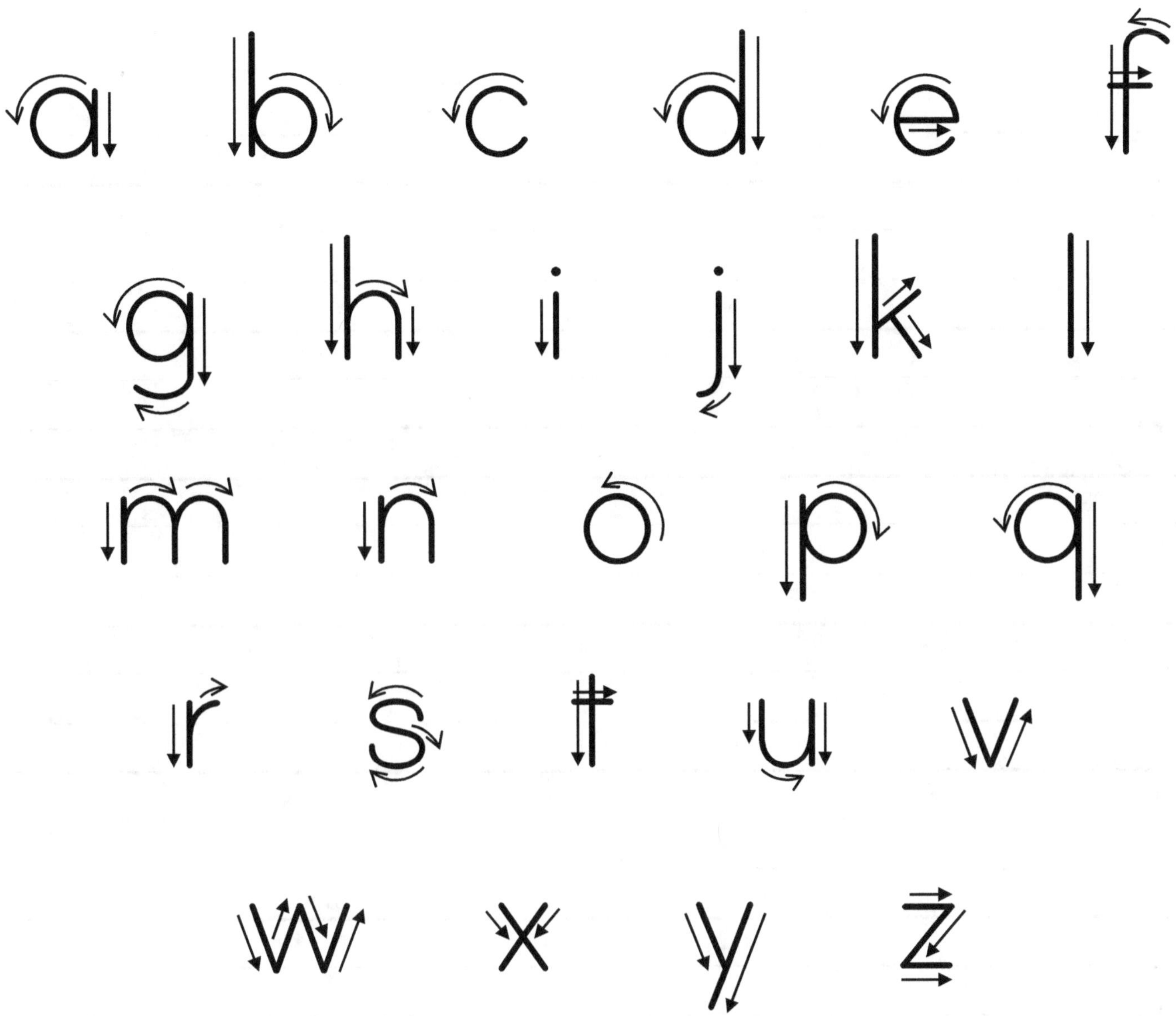

# Print letter practice

*Fact No.1*

Venus and Mercury are the only two planets in
our solar system that have no moons.

Venus

Mercury

planets

moons

Copy the entire previous quote below while using your best handwriting.

# Venus is the hottest planet in our solar system.

hottest

planet

solar

system

Copy the entire previous quote below while using your best handwriting.

Scientists estimate that the Sun will expand and become a red giant in approximately 5 billion years.

red

giant

billion

years

Copy the entire previous quote below while using your best handwriting.

*Fact No. 4*

The highest mountain known to man is called Olympus Mons and is located on Mars. Its peak is 16 miles high (25 kilometers), making it almost 3 times as tall as Mount Everest.

Olympus

Mons

located

Mars

Copy the entire previous quote below while using your best handwriting.

# A light-year is defined by the distance covered by light in a single year.

distance

light

single

year

Copy the entire previous quote below while using your best handwriting.

# Our solar system is found in the Milky Way, a galaxy that is 105,700 light-years wide.

Milky

Way

galaxy

wide

Copy the entire previous quote below while using your best handwriting.

# The Earth is approximately 330,000 times lighter than the Sun.

Earth

times

lighter

Sun

Copy the entire previous quote below while using your best handwriting.

Jupiter has a total of 79 moons, making it the planet with the most moons in our solar system.

Jupiter

making

most

moons

Copy the entire previous quote below while using your best handwriting.

*Fact No.9*

The largest moon in our solar system is called
Ganymede. It orbits Jupiter and is 33,279 miles
(5,262 km) in diameter.

called

Ganymede

orbits

diameter

Copy the entire previous quote below while using your best handwriting.

One day on Mars is approximately 24 hours, 39 minutes, and 35 seconds long.

One

day

minutes

seconds

Copy the entire previous quote below while using your best handwriting.

# The Sun rotates on its axis once every 25 to 35 days.

rotates

axis

once

every

Copy the entire previous quote below while using your best handwriting.

Earth is the only planet in our solar system not named after a Roman god or goddess.

named

after

Roman

goddess

Copy the entire previous quote below while using your best handwriting.

Venus is the planet in our solar system with the most volcanoes.

Venus

with

most

volcanoes

Copy the entire previous quote below while using your best handwriting.

Uranus has a blue glow because its atmosphere is made up of methane, hydrogen, and helium.

blue

glow

hydrogen

helium

Copy the entire previous quote below while using your best handwriting.

The only gas giants in our solar system are Jupiter, Saturn, Uranus, and Neptune.

Jupiter

Saturn

Uranus

Neptune

Copy the entire previous quote below while using your best handwriting.

# A season on the planet Uranus is equal to 21 years on Earth.

season

planet

equal

years

Copy the entire previous quote below while using your best handwriting.

There are more stars in the Universe than there are grains of sand on the Earth.

more

stars

grains

sand

Copy the entire previous quote below while using your best handwriting.

*Fact No.18*

# So far, the International Space Station is the largest manned object ever sent into space.

far

Space

Station

largest

Copy the entire previous quote below while using your best handwriting.

# One day on Pluto lasts approximately 153.6 hours.

day

Pluto

lasts

hours

Copy the entire previous quote below while using your best handwriting.

Outer space is generally considered to lie at an altitude of 62 miles (100 kilometers) above sea level.

Outer

generally

altitude

above

Copy the entire previous quote below while using your best handwriting.

There are between 100 and 400 billion stars within the Milky Way galaxy.

between

billion

stars

within

Copy the entire previous quote below while using your best handwriting.

Venus has sulfuric acid rains and metal snows. These extraordinary weather conditions are the result of the planet's atmospheric composition and extreme heat.

sulfuric

rains

metal

snows

Copy the entire previous quote below while using your best handwriting.

# Saturn would float in water because it's mostly made out of gas.

float

water

mostly

gas

Copy the entire previous quote below while using your best handwriting.

*Fact No.24*

# A Martian sunset appears blue.

Martian

sunset

appears

blue

Copy the entire previous quote below while using your best handwriting.

# The Earth is about 81 times heavier than the Moon.

about

times

heavier

Moon

Copy the entire previous quote below while using your best handwriting.

# Mercury has almost no atmosphere.

Mercury

almost

no

atmosphere

Copy the entire previous quote below while using your best handwriting.

# Red dwarf stars can burn continually for up to 10 trillion years.

Red

dwarf

burn

continually

Copy the entire previous quote below while using your best handwriting.

# You cannot write in space with normal pens due to the lack of gravity.

cannot

write

space

pens

Copy the entire previous quote below while using your best handwriting.

# Light travels from the Moon to the Earth in about 1.3 seconds.

Light

travels

from

seconds

Copy the entire previous quote below while using your best handwriting.

# Pluto was reclassified in 2006 as a dwarf planet.

Pluto

reclassified

dwarf

planet

Copy the entire previous quote below while using your best handwriting.

Meteoroids are much smaller than asteroids. Their size ranges from small grains to one-meter-wide objects.

Meteoroids

asteroids

grains

objects

Copy the entire previous quote below while using your best handwriting.

# The Sun is about 4.6 billion years old.

Sun

about

years

old

Copy the entire previous quote below while using your best handwriting.

The Sun's core can reach temperatures of more than 27 million degrees Fahrenheit (15 million degrees Celsius).

core

degrees

Fahrenheit

Celsius

Copy the entire previous quote below while using your best handwriting.

# The Milky Way and Andromeda galaxies will collide in about 4.5 billion years.

Andromeda

galaxies

will

collide

Copy the entire previous quote below while using your best handwriting.

*Fact No.35*

# It is believed that the Universe is around 13.8 billion years old.

believed

Universe

billion

old

Copy the entire previous quote below while using your best handwriting.

# Our solar system is about 4.57 billion years old.

solar

system

billion

years

Copy the entire previous quote below while using your best handwriting.

*Fact No.37*

# A star can be torn apart if it draws too close to a black hole.

apart

draws

black

hole

Copy the entire previous quote below while using your best handwriting.

Because there is no wind on the Moon, the footprints left by astronauts will never disappear.

wind

footprints

astronauts

disappear

Copy the entire previous quote below while using your best handwriting.

# Pluto is smaller than the Earth's moon.

Pluto

smaller

Earth's

moon

Copy the entire previous quote below while using your best handwriting.

Neptune orbits the Sun in nearly 165 Earth years.

Neptune

orbits

in

nearly

Copy the entire previous quote below while using your best handwriting.

The second-largest planet in our solar system is Saturn. Its diameter is nine times that of Earth's.

Saturn

Its

nine

times

Copy the entire previous quote below while using your best handwriting.

The largest planet in our solar system is Jupiter. Its diameter is eleven times that of Earth's.

largest

planet

Jupiter

eleven

Copy the entire previous quote below while using your best handwriting.

Light travels from the Sun to the Earth's surface in about 8 minutes and 20 seconds.

Light

travels

from

surface

Copy the entire previous quote below while using your best handwriting.

The closest spiral galaxy to ours is the Andromeda Galaxy. It is approximately 2.5 million light-years away.

closest

spiral

ours

away

Copy the entire previous quote below while using your best handwriting.

# Planets that orbit other stars are called "exoplanets."

orbit

stars

called

exoplanets

Copy the entire previous quote below while using your best handwriting.